MW01169411

Copy

First printing, Jan 2021
Copyright © 2021

Disclaimer

More Journals!

Want a Journal to give your busy friend or family member as a gift, or just want more Journal ideas?

Check out some of our other Journals...

90 Day Better Career Journal
90 Day Daily Positivity Journal
90 Day Self Discovery Journal
90 Day Healthy Habit Journal
90 Day Mental Health Journal
Your 90 Day Daily Victory Journal
Your 365 Day Wellbeing Journal

Choose from different lengths (60 days, 90 days and yearly) as well as different types of journals (with different goals and objectives). You are sure to find something that'll be great both as a personal journal and as a gift!

Free Gift!

Want a free gift?

Email us at
betterlifejournals@gmail.com

Title the email "Journal" and we will send you
something fun!

Visit our website for more:
https://lifelabmagazine.com/better-life-
journals/

THE
WHEEL OF
LIFE
WORKBOOK

Your Daily Life Improvement and
Self Care Workbook & Journal for
a Happier, Healthier and more
Balanced Life

GETTING STARTED

The workbook and journal is pretty self-explanatory so you can just go through it at your own pace. That said, here are some pointers that can help you get the most out of this:

- **Complete the wheel of life exercise and goals section** before you begin. This will help you get some valuable insight and clarity about how balanced your life is right now and what needs work.
- **Set out a time** in the day when you will commit to completing the daily pages over the coming days. Having a specific time will help you stay on course. An easy way is to schedule a recurring reminder on your phone's calendar.
- Complete the daily journal pages as honestly as possible. This is your personal journey, not something you are doing to show others, and personal honesty is vital to improving the quality of your life.

Most importantly, take it one day at a time. Small actions overtime will get you big results, as you will soon find out :)

When we strive to become better than we are, everything around us becomes better too

Paulo Coelho

WHEEL OF LIFE

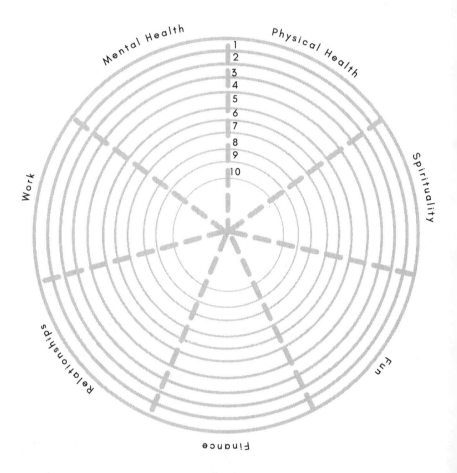

Mental Health · Physical Health · Spirituality · Fun · Finance · Relationships · Work

1 2 3 4 5 6 7 8 9 10

DATE:

Honestly score each of the areas of your life on the wheel based on where you believe you are right now.

This is the beginning. Once you have finished this workbook complete the one at the end to compare your progress.

LIFE IMPROVEMENT PLAN

Pick the areas of your life you want to improve. Now think, why is it important for you to improve them, and how can you improve these areas? Jot down as many ideas as you can. You can then use these ideas to plan your big goals (next page), as well as the daily tasks.

90 DAY GOALS

What areas of your life would you like to improve, why, and by how much (pick a maximum of 3)?

Tip: Don't overwhelm yourself. It is understandable if you are excited about improving different areas of your life, but it is better to focus on less than more. That way you can always do more if you have time and energy, but if you don't you it will still be ok as you will still make progress.

What is your main goal for the next 90 days (something you would be happy about accomplishing even if that is the only thing you accomplish)? Why is this goal important?

DATE: MOOD: ★ ★ ★ ★ ★

WHAT'S ON MY MIND RIGHT NOW?
✏

GRATITUDE LOG:

MAIN GOALS:

MY AFFIRMATION OF THE DAY...

HAPPINESS CHECKLIST

PHYSICAL:
● Exercise
●
●
●
●

EMOTIONAL:
● Mindfulness
●
●
●
●

SPIRITUAL:
● Meditate
●
●
●
●

WORK:
● Plan my day
●
●
●
●

FINANCE:
● Track exps
●
●
●
●

SOCIAL:
● Connect
●
●
●
●

DATE: **MOOD:** ★ ★ ★ ★ ★

WHAT'S ON MY MIND RIGHT NOW?

GRATITUDE LOG:

MAIN GOALS:

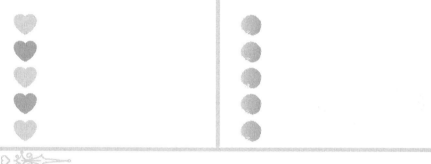

MY AFFIRMATION OF THE DAY...

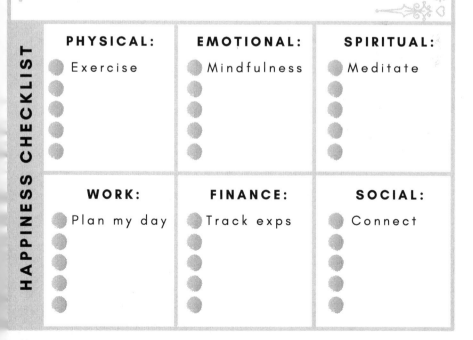

HAPPINESS CHECKLIST

PHYSICAL:
- Exercise
-
-
-
-

EMOTIONAL:
- Mindfulness
-
-
-
-

SPIRITUAL:
- Meditate
-
-
-
-

WORK:
- Plan my day
-
-
-
-

FINANCE:
- Track exps
-
-
-
-

SOCIAL:
- Connect
-
-
-
-

DATE: MOOD: ★ ★ ★ ★ ★

WHAT'S ON MY MIND RIGHT NOW?

GRATITUDE LOG:

MAIN GOALS:

MY AFFIRMATION OF THE DAY...

HAPPINESS CHECKLIST

PHYSICAL:
Exercise

EMOTIONAL:
Mindfulness

SPIRITUAL:
Meditate

WORK:
Plan my day

FINANCE:
Track exps

SOCIAL:
Connect

DATE:

MOOD: ★ ★ ★ ★ ★

WHAT'S ON MY MIND RIGHT NOW?

GRATITUDE LOG:

MAIN GOALS:

MY AFFIRMATION OF THE DAY...

HAPPINESS CHECKLIST

PHYSICAL:
Exercise

EMOTIONAL:
Mindfulness

SPIRITUAL:
Meditate

WORK:
Plan my day

FINANCE:
Track exps

SOCIAL:
Connect

DATE:

MOOD: ★ ★ ★ ★ ★

WHAT'S ON MY MIND RIGHT NOW?

GRATITUDE LOG:

MAIN GOALS:

MY AFFIRMATION OF THE DAY...

HAPPINESS CHECKLIST

PHYSICAL:
- Exercise
-
-
-
-

EMOTIONAL:
- Mindfulness
-
-
-
-

SPIRITUAL:
- Meditate
-
-
-
-

WORK:
- Plan my day
-
-
-
-

FINANCE:
- Track exps
-
-
-
-

SOCIAL:
- Connect
-
-
-
-

DATE:

MOOD: ⭐ ⭐ ⭐ ⭐ ⭐

WHAT'S ON MY MIND RIGHT NOW?

GRATITUDE LOG:

MAIN GOALS:

MY AFFIRMATION OF THE DAY...

HAPPINESS CHECKLIST

PHYSICAL:
- Exercise
-
-
-
-

EMOTIONAL:
- Mindfulness
-
-
-
-

SPIRITUAL:
- Meditate
-
-
-
-

WORK:
- Plan my day
-
-
-
-

FINANCE:
- Track exps
-
-
-
-

SOCIAL:
- Connect
-
-
-
-

DATE: **MOOD:** ★ ★ ★ ★ ★

WHAT'S ON MY MIND RIGHT NOW?

GRATITUDE LOG:

MAIN GOALS:

MY AFFIRMATION OF THE DAY...

HAPPINESS CHECKLIST

PHYSICAL:
- Exercise

EMOTIONAL:
- Mindfulness

SPIRITUAL:
- Meditate

WORK:
- Plan my day

FINANCE:
- Track exps

SOCIAL:
- Connect

DATE: MOOD: ⭐ ⭐ ⭐ ⭐ ⭐

WHAT'S ON MY MIND RIGHT NOW?

GRATITUDE LOG:

MAIN GOALS:

MY AFFIRMATION OF THE DAY...

HAPPINESS CHECKLIST

PHYSICAL:
- Exercise

EMOTIONAL:
- Mindfulness

SPIRITUAL:
- Meditate

WORK:
- Plan my day

FINANCE:
- Track exps

SOCIAL:
- Connect

DATE:

MOOD: ★ ★ ★ ★ ★

WHAT'S ON MY MIND RIGHT NOW?

GRATITUDE LOG:

MAIN GOALS:

MY AFFIRMATION OF THE DAY...

HAPPINESS CHECKLIST

PHYSICAL:
- Exercise

EMOTIONAL:
- Mindfulness

SPIRITUAL:
- Meditate

WORK:
- Plan my day

FINANCE:
- Track exps

SOCIAL:
- Connect

DATE: MOOD: ★ ★ ★ ★ ★

WHAT'S ON MY MIND RIGHT NOW?

GRATITUDE LOG:

MAIN GOALS:

MY AFFIRMATION OF THE DAY...

HAPPINESS CHECKLIST

PHYSICAL:
- Exercise
-
-
-
-

EMOTIONAL:
- Mindfulness
-
-
-
-

SPIRITUAL:
- Meditate
-
-
-
-

WORK:
- Plan my day
-
-
-
-

FINANCE:
- Track exps
-
-
-
-

SOCIAL:
- Connect
-
-
-
-

DATE: MOOD: ★ ★ ★ ★ ★

WHAT'S ON MY MIND RIGHT NOW?

GRATITUDE LOG:

MAIN GOALS:

MY AFFIRMATION OF THE DAY...

HAPPINESS CHECKLIST

PHYSICAL:
- Exercise

EMOTIONAL:
- Mindfulness

SPIRITUAL:
- Meditate

WORK:
- Plan my day

FINANCE:
- Track exps

SOCIAL:
- Connect

DATE:

MOOD: ⭐ ⭐ ⭐ ⭐ ⭐

WHAT'S ON MY MIND RIGHT NOW?

GRATITUDE LOG:

MAIN GOALS:

MY AFFIRMATION OF THE DAY...

HAPPINESS CHECKLIST

PHYSICAL:
- Exercise

EMOTIONAL:
- Mindfulness

SPIRITUAL:
- Meditate

WORK:
- Plan my day

FINANCE:
- Track exps

SOCIAL:
- Connect

DATE: MOOD: ★ ★ ★ ★ ★

WHAT'S ON MY MIND RIGHT NOW?

GRATITUDE LOG:

MAIN GOALS:

MY AFFIRMATION OF THE DAY...

HAPPINESS CHECKLIST

PHYSICAL:
- Exercise

EMOTIONAL:
- Mindfulness

SPIRITUAL:
- Meditate

WORK:
- Plan my day

FINANCE:
- Track exps

SOCIAL:
- Connect

DATE:

MOOD: ★ ★ ★ ★ ★

WHAT'S ON MY MIND RIGHT NOW?

GRATITUDE LOG:

MAIN GOALS:

MY AFFIRMATION OF THE DAY...

HAPPINESS CHECKLIST

PHYSICAL:
- Exercise

EMOTIONAL:
- Mindfulness

SPIRITUAL:
- Meditate

WORK:
- Plan my day

FINANCE:
- Track exps

SOCIAL:
- Connect

DATE: MOOD: ★ ★ ★ ★ ★

WHAT'S ON MY MIND RIGHT NOW?

GRATITUDE LOG:

MAIN GOALS:

MY AFFIRMATION OF THE DAY...

HAPPINESS CHECKLIST

PHYSICAL:
- Exercise

EMOTIONAL:
- Mindfulness

SPIRITUAL:
- Meditate

WORK:
- Plan my day

FINANCE:
- Track exps

SOCIAL:
- Connect

DATE: MOOD: ⭐ ⭐ ⭐ ⭐ ⭐

WHAT'S ON MY MIND RIGHT NOW?

GRATITUDE LOG:

MAIN GOALS:

MY AFFIRMATION OF THE DAY...

HAPPINESS CHECKLIST

PHYSICAL:
Exercise

EMOTIONAL:
Mindfulness

SPIRITUAL:
Meditate

WORK:
Plan my day

FINANCE:
Track exps

SOCIAL:
Connect

DATE:

MOOD: ★ ★ ★ ★ ★

WHAT'S ON MY MIND RIGHT NOW?

GRATITUDE LOG:

MAIN GOALS:

MY AFFIRMATION OF THE DAY...

HAPPINESS CHECKLIST

PHYSICAL:
- Exercise
-
-
-
-

EMOTIONAL:
- Mindfulness
-
-
-
-

SPIRITUAL:
- Meditate
-
-
-
-

WORK:
- Plan my day
-
-
-
-

FINANCE:
- Track exps
-
-
-
-

SOCIAL:
- Connect
-
-
-
-

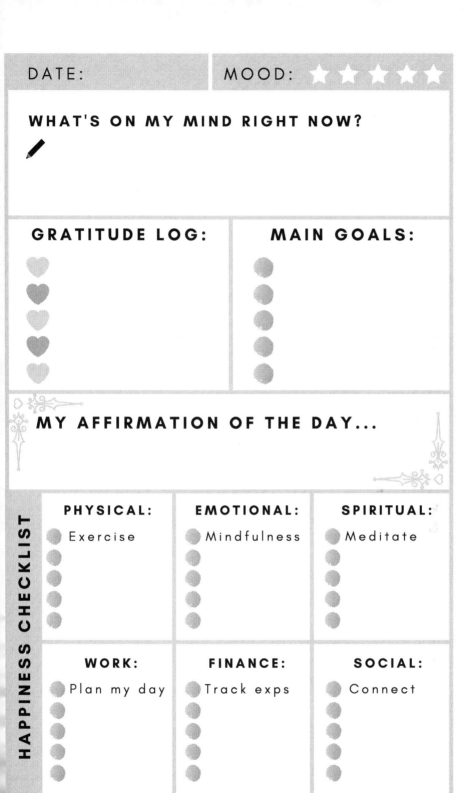

DATE: MOOD: ⭐ ⭐ ⭐ ⭐ ⭐

WHAT'S ON MY MIND RIGHT NOW?

GRATITUDE LOG:

MAIN GOALS:

MY AFFIRMATION OF THE DAY...

HAPPINESS CHECKLIST

PHYSICAL:
- Exercise

EMOTIONAL:
- Mindfulness

SPIRITUAL:
- Meditate

WORK:
- Plan my day

FINANCE:
- Track exps

SOCIAL:
- Connect

DATE: **MOOD:** ★ ★ ★ ★ ★

WHAT'S ON MY MIND RIGHT NOW?

GRATITUDE LOG:

MAIN GOALS:

MY AFFIRMATION OF THE DAY...

HAPPINESS CHECKLIST

PHYSICAL:
● Exercise
●
●
●
●

EMOTIONAL:
● Mindfulness
●
●
●
●

SPIRITUAL:
● Meditate
●
●
●
●

WORK:
● Plan my day
●
●
●
●

FINANCE:
● Track exps
●
●
●
●

SOCIAL:
● Connect
●
●
●
●

DATE:

MOOD: ⭐ ⭐ ⭐ ⭐ ⭐

WHAT'S ON MY MIND RIGHT NOW?

GRATITUDE LOG:

MAIN GOALS:

MY AFFIRMATION OF THE DAY...

HAPPINESS CHECKLIST

PHYSICAL:
- Exercise
-
-
-
-

EMOTIONAL:
- Mindfulness
-
-
-
-

SPIRITUAL:
- Meditate
-
-
-
-

WORK:
- Plan my day
-
-
-
-

FINANCE:
- Track exps
-
-
-
-

SOCIAL:
- Connect
-
-
-
-

DATE:

MOOD: ★ ★ ★ ★ ★

WHAT'S ON MY MIND RIGHT NOW?

GRATITUDE LOG:

MAIN GOALS:

MY AFFIRMATION OF THE DAY...

HAPPINESS CHECKLIST

PHYSICAL:
- Exercise
-
-
-
-

EMOTIONAL:
- Mindfulness
-
-
-
-

SPIRITUAL:
- Meditate
-
-
-
-

WORK:
- Plan my day
-
-
-
-

FINANCE:
- Track exps
-
-
-
-

SOCIAL:
- Connect
-
-
-
-

DATE: MOOD: ★ ★ ★ ★ ★

WHAT'S ON MY MIND RIGHT NOW?

GRATITUDE LOG:

MAIN GOALS:

MY AFFIRMATION OF THE DAY...

HAPPINESS CHECKLIST

PHYSICAL:
- Exercise
-
-
-
-

EMOTIONAL:
- Mindfulness
-
-
-
-

SPIRITUAL:
- Meditate
-
-
-
-

WORK:
- Plan my day
-
-
-
-

FINANCE:
- Track exps
-
-
-
-

SOCIAL:
- Connect
-
-
-
-

DATE: MOOD: ★ ★ ★ ★ ★

WHAT'S ON MY MIND RIGHT NOW?

GRATITUDE LOG:

MAIN GOALS:

MY AFFIRMATION OF THE DAY...

HAPPINESS CHECKLIST

PHYSICAL:
- Exercise
-
-
-
-

EMOTIONAL:
- Mindfulness
-
-
-
-

SPIRITUAL:
- Meditate
-
-
-
-

WORK:
- Plan my day
-
-
-
-

FINANCE:
- Track exps
-
-
-
-

SOCIAL:
- Connect
-
-
-
-

DATE:

MOOD: ⭐ ⭐ ⭐ ⭐ ⭐

WHAT'S ON MY MIND RIGHT NOW?

GRATITUDE LOG:

MAIN GOALS:

MY AFFIRMATION OF THE DAY...

HAPPINESS CHECKLIST

PHYSICAL:
- Exercise
-
-
-
-

EMOTIONAL:
- Mindfulness
-
-
-
-

SPIRITUAL:
- Meditate
-
-
-
-

WORK:
- Plan my day
-
-
-
-

FINANCE:
- Track exps
-
-
-
-

SOCIAL:
- Connect
-
-
-
-

DATE: MOOD: ★ ★ ★ ★ ★

WHAT'S ON MY MIND RIGHT NOW?

GRATITUDE LOG:

MAIN GOALS:

MY AFFIRMATION OF THE DAY...

HAPPINESS CHECKLIST

PHYSICAL:
- Exercise
-
-
-
-

EMOTIONAL:
- Mindfulness
-
-
-
-

SPIRITUAL:
- Meditate
-
-
-
-

WORK:
- Plan my day
-
-
-
-

FINANCE:
- Track exps
-
-
-
-

SOCIAL:
- Connect
-
-
-
-

DATE: MOOD:

WHAT'S ON MY MIND RIGHT NOW?

GRATITUDE LOG:

MAIN GOALS:

MY AFFIRMATION OF THE DAY...

HAPPINESS CHECKLIST

PHYSICAL:
- Exercise

EMOTIONAL:
- Mindfulness

SPIRITUAL:
- Meditate

WORK:
- Plan my day

FINANCE:
- Track exps

SOCIAL:
- Connect

DATE: MOOD: ★ ★ ★ ★ ★

WHAT'S ON MY MIND RIGHT NOW?

GRATITUDE LOG:

MAIN GOALS:

MY AFFIRMATION OF THE DAY...

HAPPINESS CHECKLIST

PHYSICAL:
- Exercise
-
-
-
-

EMOTIONAL:
- Mindfulness
-
-
-
-

SPIRITUAL:
- Meditate
-
-
-
-

WORK:
- Plan my day
-
-
-
-

FINANCE:
- Track exps
-
-
-
-

SOCIAL:
- Connect
-
-
-
-

DATE:

MOOD: ★ ★ ★ ★ ★

WHAT'S ON MY MIND RIGHT NOW?

GRATITUDE LOG:

MAIN GOALS:

MY AFFIRMATION OF THE DAY...

HAPPINESS CHECKLIST

PHYSICAL:
- Exercise
-
-
-
-

EMOTIONAL:
- Mindfulness
-
-
-
-

SPIRITUAL:
- Meditate
-
-
-
-

WORK:
- Plan my day
-
-
-
-

FINANCE:
- Track exps
-
-
-
-

SOCIAL:
- Connect
-
-
-
-

DATE:

MOOD: ★ ★ ★ ★ ★

WHAT'S ON MY MIND RIGHT NOW?

GRATITUDE LOG:

MAIN GOALS:

MY AFFIRMATION OF THE DAY...

HAPPINESS CHECKLIST

PHYSICAL:
- Exercise
-
-
-
-

EMOTIONAL:
- Mindfulness
-
-
-
-

SPIRITUAL:
- Meditate
-
-
-
-

WORK:
- Plan my day
-
-
-
-

FINANCE:
- Track exps
-
-
-
-

SOCIAL:
- Connect
-
-
-
-

DATE:

MOOD: ★ ★ ★ ★ ★

WHAT'S ON MY MIND RIGHT NOW?

GRATITUDE LOG:

MAIN GOALS:

MY AFFIRMATION OF THE DAY...

HAPPINESS CHECKLIST

PHYSICAL:
- Exercise

EMOTIONAL:
- Mindfulness

SPIRITUAL:
- Meditate

WORK:
- Plan my day

FINANCE:
- Track exps

SOCIAL:
- Connect

DATE: MOOD: ★ ★ ★ ★ ★

WHAT'S ON MY MIND RIGHT NOW?

GRATITUDE LOG:

MAIN GOALS:

MY AFFIRMATION OF THE DAY...

HAPPINESS CHECKLIST

PHYSICAL:
- Exercise
-
-
-
-

EMOTIONAL:
- Mindfulness
-
-
-
-

SPIRITUAL:
- Meditate
-
-
-
-

WORK:
- Plan my day
-
-
-
-

FINANCE:
- Track exps
-
-
-
-

SOCIAL:
- Connect
-
-
-
-

DATE: MOOD: ★ ★ ★ ★ ★

WHAT'S ON MY MIND RIGHT NOW?

GRATITUDE LOG:

MAIN GOALS:

MY AFFIRMATION OF THE DAY...

HAPPINESS CHECKLIST

PHYSICAL:
- Exercise
-
-
-
-

EMOTIONAL:
- Mindfulness
-
-
-
-

SPIRITUAL:
- Meditate
-
-
-
-

WORK:
- Plan my day
-
-
-
-

FINANCE:
- Track exps
-
-
-
-

SOCIAL:
- Connect
-
-
-
-

DATE: MOOD: ★ ★ ★ ★ ★

WHAT'S ON MY MIND RIGHT NOW?

GRATITUDE LOG:

MAIN GOALS:

MY AFFIRMATION OF THE DAY...

HAPPINESS CHECKLIST

PHYSICAL:
Exercise

EMOTIONAL:
Mindfulness

SPIRITUAL:
Meditate

WORK:
Plan my day

FINANCE:
Track exps

SOCIAL:
Connect

DATE:  MOOD:

WHAT'S ON MY MIND RIGHT NOW?

GRATITUDE LOG:

MAIN GOALS:

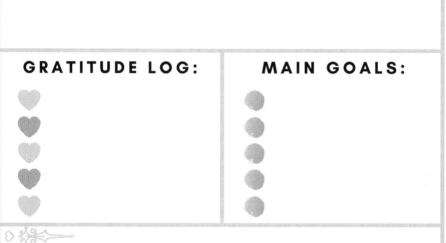

MY AFFIRMATION OF THE DAY...

HAPPINESS CHECKLIST

PHYSICAL:
Exercise

EMOTIONAL:
Mindfulness

SPIRITUAL:
Meditate

WORK:
Plan my day

FINANCE:
Track exps

SOCIAL:
Connect

DATE: MOOD: ★ ★ ★ ★ ★

WHAT'S ON MY MIND RIGHT NOW?

GRATITUDE LOG:

MAIN GOALS:

MY AFFIRMATION OF THE DAY...

HAPPINESS CHECKLIST

PHYSICAL:
- Exercise
-
-
-
-

EMOTIONAL:
- Mindfulness
-
-
-
-

SPIRITUAL:
- Meditate
-
-
-
-

WORK:
- Plan my day
-
-
-
-

FINANCE:
- Track exps
-
-
-
-

SOCIAL:
- Connect
-
-
-
-

DATE: **MOOD:**

WHAT'S ON MY MIND RIGHT NOW?

GRATITUDE LOG:

MAIN GOALS:

MY AFFIRMATION OF THE DAY...

HAPPINESS CHECKLIST

PHYSICAL:
- Exercise

EMOTIONAL:
- Mindfulness

SPIRITUAL:
- Meditate

WORK:
- Plan my day

FINANCE:
- Track exps

SOCIAL:
- Connect

DATE: **MOOD:** ★ ★ ★ ★ ★

WHAT'S ON MY MIND RIGHT NOW?

GRATITUDE LOG:

MAIN GOALS:

MY AFFIRMATION OF THE DAY...

HAPPINESS CHECKLIST

PHYSICAL:
Exercise

EMOTIONAL:
Mindfulness

SPIRITUAL:
Meditate

WORK:
Plan my day

FINANCE:
Track exps

SOCIAL:
Connect

DATE:

MOOD: ★ ★ ★ ★ ★

WHAT'S ON MY MIND RIGHT NOW?

GRATITUDE LOG:

MAIN GOALS:

MY AFFIRMATION OF THE DAY...

HAPPINESS CHECKLIST

PHYSICAL:
- Exercise
-
-
-
-

EMOTIONAL:
- Mindfulness
-
-
-
-

SPIRITUAL:
- Meditate
-
-
-
-

WORK:
- Plan my day
-
-
-
-

FINANCE:
- Track exps
-
-
-
-

SOCIAL:
- Connect
-
-
-
-

DATE:

MOOD: ★ ★ ★ ★ ★

WHAT'S ON MY MIND RIGHT NOW?

GRATITUDE LOG:

MAIN GOALS:

MY AFFIRMATION OF THE DAY...

HAPPINESS CHECKLIST

PHYSICAL:
- Exercise
-
-
-
-

EMOTIONAL:
- Mindfulness
-
-
-
-

SPIRITUAL:
- Meditate
-
-
-
-

WORK:
- Plan my day
-
-
-
-

FINANCE:
- Track exps
-
-
-
-

SOCIAL:
- Connect
-
-
-
-

DATE:

MOOD: ★ ★ ★ ★ ★

WHAT'S ON MY MIND RIGHT NOW?

GRATITUDE LOG:

MAIN GOALS:

MY AFFIRMATION OF THE DAY...

HAPPINESS CHECKLIST

PHYSICAL:
- Exercise

EMOTIONAL:
- Mindfulness

SPIRITUAL:
- Meditate

WORK:
- Plan my day

FINANCE:
- Track exps

SOCIAL:
- Connect

DATE:

MOOD: ★ ★ ★ ★ ★

WHAT'S ON MY MIND RIGHT NOW?

GRATITUDE LOG:

MAIN GOALS:

MY AFFIRMATION OF THE DAY...

HAPPINESS CHECKLIST

PHYSICAL:
- Exercise

EMOTIONAL:
- Mindfulness

SPIRITUAL:
- Meditate

WORK:
- Plan my day

FINANCE:
- Track exps

SOCIAL:
- Connect

DATE:

MOOD: ★ ★ ★ ★ ★

WHAT'S ON MY MIND RIGHT NOW?

GRATITUDE LOG:

MAIN GOALS:

MY AFFIRMATION OF THE DAY...

HAPPINESS CHECKLIST

PHYSICAL:
- Exercise
-
-
-
-

EMOTIONAL:
- Mindfulness
-
-
-
-

SPIRITUAL:
- Meditate
-
-
-
-

WORK:
- Plan my day
-
-
-
-

FINANCE:
- Track exps
-
-
-
-

SOCIAL:
- Connect
-
-
-
-

DATE:

MOOD: ★ ★ ★ ★ ★

WHAT'S ON MY MIND RIGHT NOW?

GRATITUDE LOG:

MAIN GOALS:

MY AFFIRMATION OF THE DAY...

HAPPINESS CHECKLIST

PHYSICAL:
- Exercise

EMOTIONAL:
- Mindfulness

SPIRITUAL:
- Meditate

WORK:
- Plan my day

FINANCE:
- Track exps

SOCIAL:
- Connect

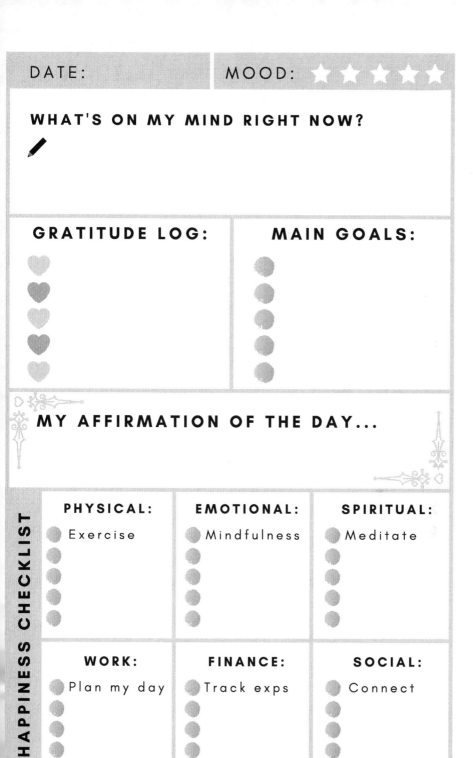

DATE:

MOOD: ★ ★ ★ ★ ★

WHAT'S ON MY MIND RIGHT NOW?

GRATITUDE LOG:

MAIN GOALS:

MY AFFIRMATION OF THE DAY...

HAPPINESS CHECKLIST

PHYSICAL:
- Exercise

EMOTIONAL:
- Mindfulness

SPIRITUAL:
- Meditate

WORK:
- Plan my day

FINANCE:
- Track exps

SOCIAL:
- Connect

DATE: MOOD: ★ ★ ★ ★ ★

WHAT'S ON MY MIND RIGHT NOW?

GRATITUDE LOG:

MAIN GOALS:

MY AFFIRMATION OF THE DAY...

HAPPINESS CHECKLIST

PHYSICAL:
- Exercise
-
-
-
-

EMOTIONAL:
- Mindfulness
-
-
-
-

SPIRITUAL:
- Meditate
-
-
-
-

WORK:
- Plan my day
-
-
-
-

FINANCE:
- Track exps
-
-
-
-

SOCIAL:
- Connect
-
-
-
-

DATE:

MOOD: ★ ★ ★ ★ ★

WHAT'S ON MY MIND RIGHT NOW?

GRATITUDE LOG:

MAIN GOALS:

MY AFFIRMATION OF THE DAY...

HAPPINESS CHECKLIST

PHYSICAL:
- Exercise

EMOTIONAL:
- Mindfulness

SPIRITUAL:
- Meditate

WORK:
- Plan my day

FINANCE:
- Track exps

SOCIAL:
- Connect

DATE: ★ **MOOD:** ★ ★ ★ ★ ★

WHAT'S ON MY MIND RIGHT NOW?

GRATITUDE LOG:

MAIN GOALS:

MY AFFIRMATION OF THE DAY...

HAPPINESS CHECKLIST

PHYSICAL:
- Exercise
-
-
-
-

EMOTIONAL:
- Mindfulness
-
-
-
-

SPIRITUAL:
- Meditate
-
-
-
-

WORK:
- Plan my day
-
-
-
-

FINANCE:
- Track exps
-
-
-
-

SOCIAL:
- Connect
-
-
-
-

DATE:

MOOD: ⭐⭐⭐⭐⭐

WHAT'S ON MY MIND RIGHT NOW?
✏️

GRATITUDE LOG:

MAIN GOALS:

MY AFFIRMATION OF THE DAY...

HAPPINESS CHECKLIST

PHYSICAL:
● Exercise
●
●
●
●

EMOTIONAL:
● Mindfulness
●
●
●
●

SPIRITUAL:
● Meditate
●
●
●
●

WORK:
● Plan my day
●
●
●
●

FINANCE:
● Track exps
●
●
●
●

SOCIAL:
● Connect
●
●
●
●

DATE:

MOOD: ★ ★ ★ ★ ★

WHAT'S ON MY MIND RIGHT NOW?

GRATITUDE LOG:

MAIN GOALS:

MY AFFIRMATION OF THE DAY...

HAPPINESS CHECKLIST

PHYSICAL:
- Exercise

EMOTIONAL:
- Mindfulness

SPIRITUAL:
- Meditate

WORK:
- Plan my day

FINANCE:
- Track exps

SOCIAL:
- Connect

DATE:

MOOD: ★ ★ ★ ★ ★

WHAT'S ON MY MIND RIGHT NOW?

GRATITUDE LOG:

MAIN GOALS:

MY AFFIRMATION OF THE DAY...

HAPPINESS CHECKLIST

PHYSICAL:
- Exercise

EMOTIONAL:
- Mindfulness

SPIRITUAL:
- Meditate

WORK:
- Plan my day

FINANCE:
- Track exps

SOCIAL:
- Connect

DATE: MOOD: ★ ★ ★ ★ ★

WHAT'S ON MY MIND RIGHT NOW?

GRATITUDE LOG:

MAIN GOALS:

MY AFFIRMATION OF THE DAY...

HAPPINESS CHECKLIST

PHYSICAL:
- Exercise

EMOTIONAL:
- Mindfulness

SPIRITUAL:
- Meditate

WORK:
- Plan my day

FINANCE:
- Track exps

SOCIAL:
- Connect

DATE: MOOD: ⭐⭐⭐⭐⭐

WHAT'S ON MY MIND RIGHT NOW?

GRATITUDE LOG:

MAIN GOALS:

MY AFFIRMATION OF THE DAY...

HAPPINESS CHECKLIST

PHYSICAL:
- Exercise
- ◯
- ◯
- ◯
- ◯

EMOTIONAL:
- Mindfulness
- ◯
- ◯
- ◯
- ◯

SPIRITUAL:
- Meditate
- ◯
- ◯
- ◯
- ◯

WORK:
- Plan my day
- ◯
- ◯
- ◯
- ◯

FINANCE:
- Track exps
- ◯
- ◯
- ◯
- ◯

SOCIAL:
- Connect
- ◯
- ◯
- ◯
- ◯

DATE: **MOOD:** ★ ★ ★ ★ ★

WHAT'S ON MY MIND RIGHT NOW?

GRATITUDE LOG:

MAIN GOALS:

MY AFFIRMATION OF THE DAY...

HAPPINESS CHECKLIST

PHYSICAL:
- Exercise
-
-
-
-

EMOTIONAL:
- Mindfulness
-
-
-
-

SPIRITUAL:
- Meditate
-
-
-
-

WORK:
- Plan my day
-
-
-
-

FINANCE:
- Track exps
-
-
-
-

SOCIAL:
- Connect
-
-
-
-

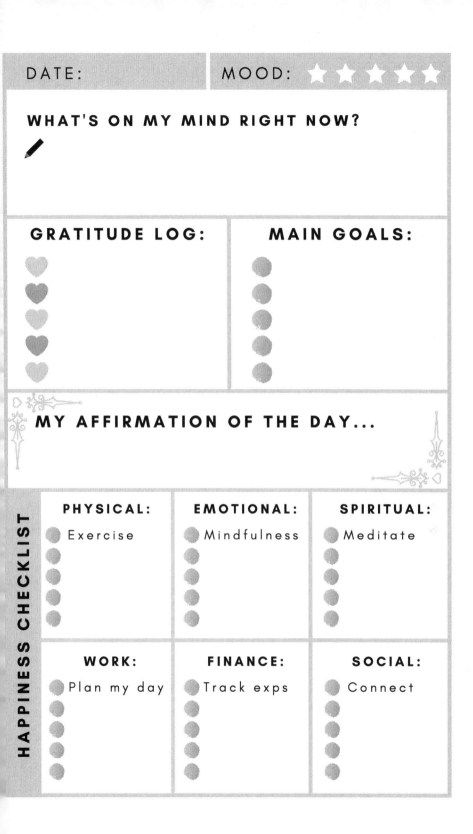

DATE:

MOOD: ★ ★ ★ ★ ★

WHAT'S ON MY MIND RIGHT NOW?

GRATITUDE LOG:

MAIN GOALS:

MY AFFIRMATION OF THE DAY...

HAPPINESS CHECKLIST

PHYSICAL:
- Exercise
-
-
-
-

EMOTIONAL:
- Mindfulness
-
-
-
-

SPIRITUAL:
- Meditate
-
-
-
-

WORK:
- Plan my day
-
-
-
-

FINANCE:
- Track exps
-
-
-
-

SOCIAL:
- Connect
-
-
-
-

DATE: MOOD: ★ ★ ★ ★ ★

WHAT'S ON MY MIND RIGHT NOW?

GRATITUDE LOG:

MAIN GOALS:

MY AFFIRMATION OF THE DAY...

HAPPINESS CHECKLIST

PHYSICAL:
- Exercise

EMOTIONAL:
- Mindfulness

SPIRITUAL:
- Meditate

WORK:
- Plan my day

FINANCE:
- Track exps

SOCIAL:
- Connect

DATE:

MOOD: ☆ ☆ ☆ ☆ ☆

WHAT'S ON MY MIND RIGHT NOW?

GRATITUDE LOG:

MAIN GOALS:

MY AFFIRMATION OF THE DAY...

HAPPINESS CHECKLIST

PHYSICAL:
- Exercise

EMOTIONAL:
- Mindfulness

SPIRITUAL:
- Meditate

WORK:
- Plan my day

FINANCE:
- Track exps

SOCIAL:
- Connect

DATE: **MOOD:** ★ ★ ★ ★ ★

WHAT'S ON MY MIND RIGHT NOW?

GRATITUDE LOG:

MAIN GOALS:

MY AFFIRMATION OF THE DAY...

HAPPINESS CHECKLIST

PHYSICAL:
Exercise

EMOTIONAL:
Mindfulness

SPIRITUAL:
Meditate

WORK:
Plan my day

FINANCE:
Track exps

SOCIAL:
Connect

DATE:

MOOD: ★ ★ ★ ★ ★

WHAT'S ON MY MIND RIGHT NOW?

GRATITUDE LOG:

MAIN GOALS:

MY AFFIRMATION OF THE DAY...

HAPPINESS CHECKLIST

PHYSICAL:
Exercise

EMOTIONAL:
Mindfulness

SPIRITUAL:
Meditate

WORK:
Plan my day

FINANCE:
Track exps

SOCIAL:
Connect

DATE:

MOOD: ★ ★ ★ ★ ★

WHAT'S ON MY MIND RIGHT NOW?

GRATITUDE LOG:

MAIN GOALS:

MY AFFIRMATION OF THE DAY...

HAPPINESS CHECKLIST

PHYSICAL:
- Exercise
-
-
-
-

EMOTIONAL:
- Mindfulness
-
-
-
-

SPIRITUAL:
- Meditate
-
-
-
-

WORK:
- Plan my day
-
-
-
-

FINANCE:
- Track exps
-
-
-
-

SOCIAL:
- Connect
-
-
-
-

DATE:

MOOD: ⭐ ⭐ ⭐ ⭐ ⭐

WHAT'S ON MY MIND RIGHT NOW?

GRATITUDE LOG:

MAIN GOALS:

MY AFFIRMATION OF THE DAY...

HAPPINESS CHECKLIST

PHYSICAL:
- Exercise
-
-
-
-

EMOTIONAL:
- Mindfulness
-
-
-
-

SPIRITUAL:
- Meditate
-
-
-
-

WORK:
- Plan my day
-
-
-
-

FINANCE:
- Track exps
-
-
-
-

SOCIAL:
- Connect
-
-
-
-

DATE:

MOOD: ★ ★ ★ ★ ★

WHAT'S ON MY MIND RIGHT NOW?

GRATITUDE LOG:

MAIN GOALS:

MY AFFIRMATION OF THE DAY...

HAPPINESS CHECKLIST

PHYSICAL:
- Exercise
-
-
-
-

EMOTIONAL:
- Mindfulness
-
-
-
-

SPIRITUAL:
- Meditate
-
-
-
-

WORK:
- Plan my day
-
-
-
-

FINANCE:
- Track exps
-
-
-
-

SOCIAL:
- Connect
-
-
-
-

DATE: **MOOD:** ★ ★ ★ ★ ★

WHAT'S ON MY MIND RIGHT NOW?

GRATITUDE LOG:

MAIN GOALS:

MY AFFIRMATION OF THE DAY...

HAPPINESS CHECKLIST

PHYSICAL:
- Exercise
-
-
-
-

EMOTIONAL:
- Mindfulness
-
-
-
-

SPIRITUAL:
- Meditate
-
-
-
-

WORK:
- Plan my day
-
-
-
-

FINANCE:
- Track exps
-
-
-
-

SOCIAL:
- Connect
-
-
-
-

DATE: **MOOD:** ★ ★ ★ ★ ★

WHAT'S ON MY MIND RIGHT NOW?

GRATITUDE LOG:

MAIN GOALS:

MY AFFIRMATION OF THE DAY...

HAPPINESS CHECKLIST

PHYSICAL:
Exercise

EMOTIONAL:
Mindfulness

SPIRITUAL:
Meditate

WORK:
Plan my day

FINANCE:
Track exps

SOCIAL:
Connect

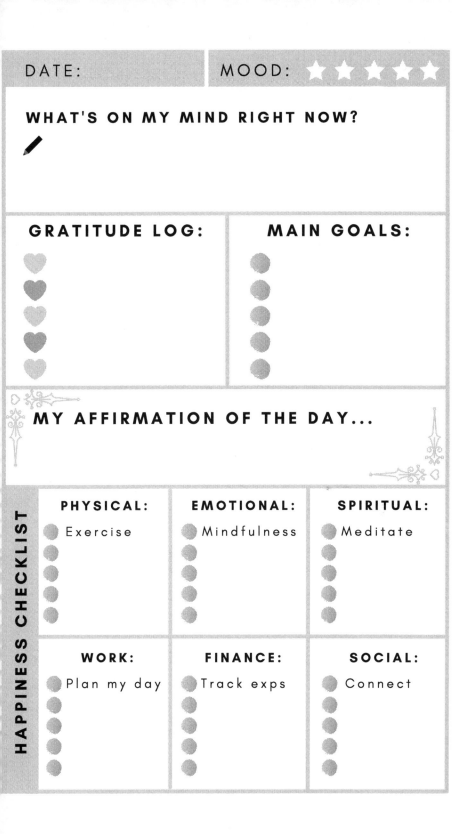

DATE:

MOOD: ⭐ ⭐ ⭐ ⭐ ⭐

WHAT'S ON MY MIND RIGHT NOW?

GRATITUDE LOG:

MAIN GOALS:

MY AFFIRMATION OF THE DAY...

HAPPINESS CHECKLIST

PHYSICAL:
- Exercise

EMOTIONAL:
- Mindfulness

SPIRITUAL:
- Meditate

WORK:
- Plan my day

FINANCE:
- Track exps

SOCIAL:
- Connect

DATE:

MOOD: ★ ★ ★ ★ ★

WHAT'S ON MY MIND RIGHT NOW?

GRATITUDE LOG:

MAIN GOALS:

MY AFFIRMATION OF THE DAY...

HAPPINESS CHECKLIST

PHYSICAL:
- Exercise
-
-
-
-

EMOTIONAL:
- Mindfulness
-
-
-
-

SPIRITUAL:
- Meditate
-
-
-
-

WORK:
- Plan my day
-
-
-
-

FINANCE:
- Track exps
-
-
-
-

SOCIAL:
- Connect
-
-
-
-

DATE: MOOD: ★ ★ ★ ★ ★

WHAT'S ON MY MIND RIGHT NOW?

GRATITUDE LOG:

MAIN GOALS:

MY AFFIRMATION OF THE DAY...

HAPPINESS CHECKLIST

PHYSICAL:
- Exercise
-
-
-
-

EMOTIONAL:
- Mindfulness
-
-
-
-

SPIRITUAL:
- Meditate
-
-
-
-

WORK:
- Plan my day
-
-
-
-

FINANCE:
- Track exps
-
-
-
-

SOCIAL:
- Connect
-
-
-
-

DATE: **MOOD:** ★ ★ ★ ★ ★

WHAT'S ON MY MIND RIGHT NOW?

GRATITUDE LOG:

MAIN GOALS:

MY AFFIRMATION OF THE DAY...

HAPPINESS CHECKLIST

PHYSICAL:
- Exercise
-
-
-
-

EMOTIONAL:
- Mindfulness
-
-
-
-

SPIRITUAL:
- Meditate
-
-
-
-

WORK:
- Plan my day
-
-
-
-

FINANCE:
- Track exps
-
-
-
-

SOCIAL:
- Connect
-
-
-
-

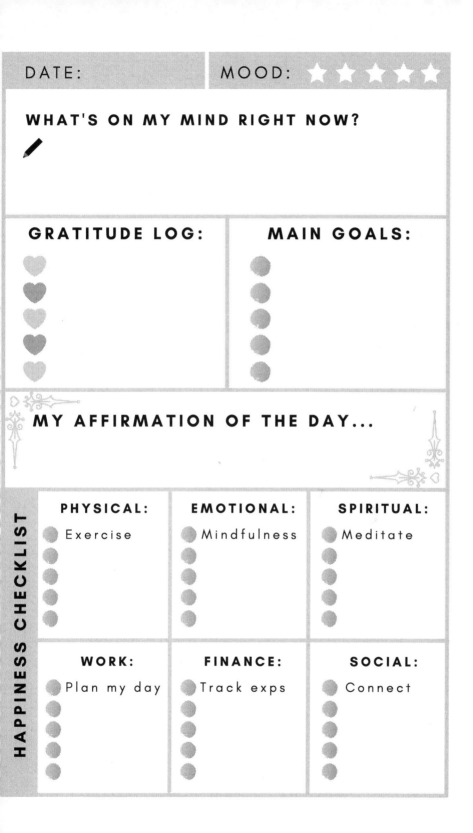

DATE: **MOOD:** ★ ★ ★ ★ ★

WHAT'S ON MY MIND RIGHT NOW?

GRATITUDE LOG:

MAIN GOALS:

MY AFFIRMATION OF THE DAY...

HAPPINESS CHECKLIST

PHYSICAL:
- Exercise
-
-
-
-

EMOTIONAL:
- Mindfulness
-
-
-
-

SPIRITUAL:
- Meditate
-
-
-
-

WORK:
- Plan my day
-
-
-
-

FINANCE:
- Track exps
-
-
-
-

SOCIAL:
- Connect
-
-
-
-

DATE:

MOOD: ★ ★ ★ ★ ★

WHAT'S ON MY MIND RIGHT NOW?

GRATITUDE LOG:

MAIN GOALS:

MY AFFIRMATION OF THE DAY...

HAPPINESS CHECKLIST

PHYSICAL:
- Exercise
-
-
-
-

EMOTIONAL:
- Mindfulness
-
-
-
-

SPIRITUAL:
- Meditate
-
-
-
-

WORK:
- Plan my day
-
-
-
-

FINANCE:
- Track exps
-
-
-
-

SOCIAL:
- Connect
-
-
-
-

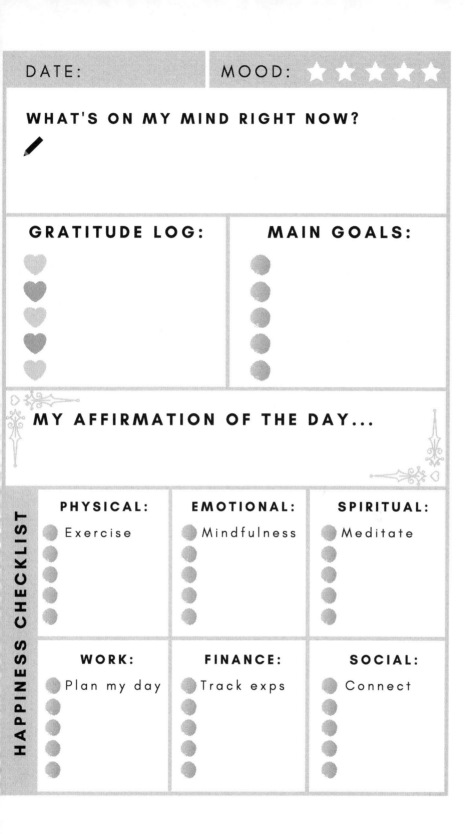

DATE:

MOOD: ★ ★ ★ ★ ★

WHAT'S ON MY MIND RIGHT NOW?

GRATITUDE LOG:

MAIN GOALS:

MY AFFIRMATION OF THE DAY...

HAPPINESS CHECKLIST

PHYSICAL:
Exercise

EMOTIONAL:
Mindfulness

SPIRITUAL:
Meditate

WORK:
Plan my day

FINANCE:
Track exps

SOCIAL:
Connect

DATE:

MOOD: ★ ★ ★ ★ ★

WHAT'S ON MY MIND RIGHT NOW?

GRATITUDE LOG:

MAIN GOALS:

MY AFFIRMATION OF THE DAY...

HAPPINESS CHECKLIST

PHYSICAL:
- Exercise

EMOTIONAL:
- Mindfulness

SPIRITUAL:
- Meditate

WORK:
- Plan my day

FINANCE:
- Track exps

SOCIAL:
- Connect

DATE: **MOOD:** ★ ★ ★ ★ ★

WHAT'S ON MY MIND RIGHT NOW?

GRATITUDE LOG:

MAIN GOALS:

MY AFFIRMATION OF THE DAY...

HAPPINESS CHECKLIST

PHYSICAL:
- Exercise
-
-
-
-

EMOTIONAL:
- Mindfulness
-
-
-
-

SPIRITUAL:
- Meditate
-
-
-
-

WORK:
- Plan my day
-
-
-
-

FINANCE:
- Track exps
-
-
-
-

SOCIAL:
- Connect
-
-
-
-

DATE: MOOD: ★ ★ ★ ★ ★

WHAT'S ON MY MIND RIGHT NOW?

GRATITUDE LOG:

MAIN GOALS:

MY AFFIRMATION OF THE DAY...

HAPPINESS CHECKLIST

PHYSICAL:
- Exercise
-
-
-
-

EMOTIONAL:
- Mindfulness
-
-
-
-

SPIRITUAL:
- Meditate
-
-
-
-

WORK:
- Plan my day
-
-
-
-

FINANCE:
- Track exps
-
-
-
-

SOCIAL:
- Connect
-
-
-
-

DATE:

MOOD: ★ ★ ★ ★ ★

WHAT'S ON MY MIND RIGHT NOW?

GRATITUDE LOG:

MAIN GOALS:

MY AFFIRMATION OF THE DAY...

HAPPINESS CHECKLIST

PHYSICAL:
- Exercise

EMOTIONAL:
- Mindfulness

SPIRITUAL:
- Meditate

WORK:
- Plan my day

FINANCE:
- Track exps

SOCIAL:
- Connect

DATE:

MOOD: ★ ★ ★ ★ ★

WHAT'S ON MY MIND RIGHT NOW?

GRATITUDE LOG:

MAIN GOALS:

MY AFFIRMATION OF THE DAY...

HAPPINESS CHECKLIST

PHYSICAL:
- Exercise
-
-
-
-

EMOTIONAL:
- Mindfulness
-
-
-
-

SPIRITUAL:
- Meditate
-
-
-
-

WORK:
- Plan my day
-
-
-
-

FINANCE:
- Track exps
-
-
-
-

SOCIAL:
- Connect
-
-
-
-

DATE:

MOOD: ⭐ ⭐ ⭐ ⭐ ⭐

WHAT'S ON MY MIND RIGHT NOW?

GRATITUDE LOG:

MAIN GOALS:

MY AFFIRMATION OF THE DAY...

HAPPINESS CHECKLIST

PHYSICAL:
- Exercise

EMOTIONAL:
- Mindfulness

SPIRITUAL:
- Meditate

WORK:
- Plan my day

FINANCE:
- Track exps

SOCIAL:
- Connect

DATE: **MOOD:** ★ ★ ★ ★ ★

WHAT'S ON MY MIND RIGHT NOW?

GRATITUDE LOG:

MAIN GOALS:

MY AFFIRMATION OF THE DAY...

HAPPINESS CHECKLIST

PHYSICAL:
- Exercise

EMOTIONAL:
- Mindfulness

SPIRITUAL:
- Meditate

WORK:
- Plan my day

FINANCE:
- Track exps

SOCIAL:
- Connect

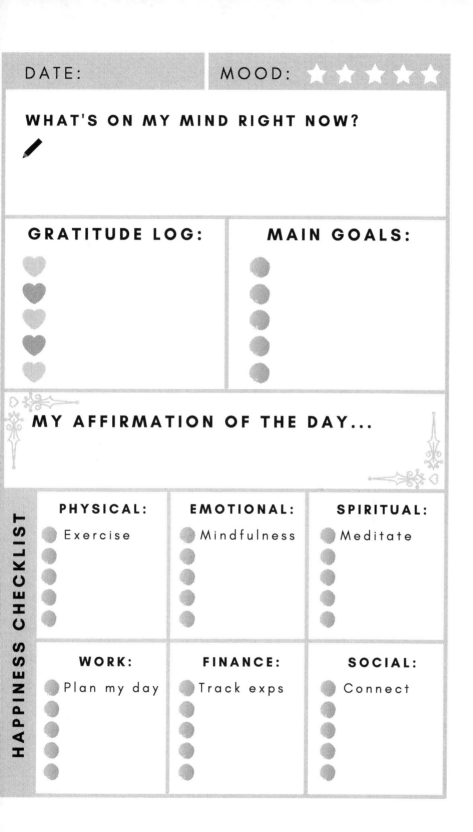

DATE:

MOOD: ★ ★ ★ ★ ★

WHAT'S ON MY MIND RIGHT NOW?

GRATITUDE LOG:

MAIN GOALS:

MY AFFIRMATION OF THE DAY...

HAPPINESS CHECKLIST

PHYSICAL:
- Exercise
-
-
-
-

EMOTIONAL:
- Mindfulness
-
-
-
-

SPIRITUAL:
- Meditate
-
-
-
-

WORK:
- Plan my day
-
-
-
-

FINANCE:
- Track exps
-
-
-
-

SOCIAL:
- Connect
-
-
-
-

DATE: **MOOD:** ★ ★ ★ ★ ★

WHAT'S ON MY MIND RIGHT NOW?

GRATITUDE LOG:

MAIN GOALS:

MY AFFIRMATION OF THE DAY...

HAPPINESS CHECKLIST

PHYSICAL:
- Exercise

EMOTIONAL:
- Mindfulness

SPIRITUAL:
- Meditate

WORK:
- Plan my day

FINANCE:
- Track exps

SOCIAL:
- Connect

DATE: MOOD: ★ ★ ★ ★ ★

WHAT'S ON MY MIND RIGHT NOW?

GRATITUDE LOG:

MAIN GOALS:

MY AFFIRMATION OF THE DAY...

HAPPINESS CHECKLIST

PHYSICAL:
- Exercise
-
-
-
-

EMOTIONAL:
- Mindfulness
-
-
-
-

SPIRITUAL:
- Meditate
-
-
-
-

WORK:
- Plan my day
-
-
-
-

FINANCE:
- Track exps
-
-
-
-

SOCIAL:
- Connect
-
-
-
-

DATE: | MOOD: ★ ★ ★ ★ ★

WHAT'S ON MY MIND RIGHT NOW?

GRATITUDE LOG:

MAIN GOALS:

MY AFFIRMATION OF THE DAY...

HAPPINESS CHECKLIST

PHYSICAL:
Exercise

EMOTIONAL:
Mindfulness

SPIRITUAL:
Meditate

WORK:
Plan my day

FINANCE:
Track exps

SOCIAL:
Connect

DATE:

MOOD: ★ ★ ★ ★ ★

WHAT'S ON MY MIND RIGHT NOW?

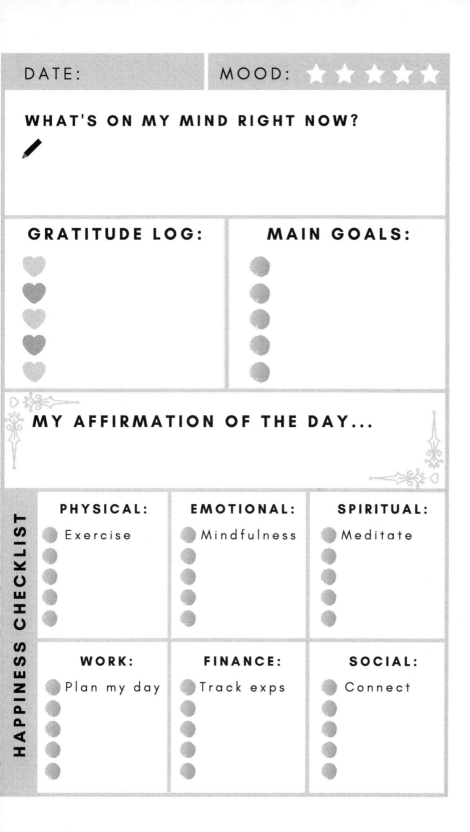

GRATITUDE LOG:

MAIN GOALS:

MY AFFIRMATION OF THE DAY...

HAPPINESS CHECKLIST

PHYSICAL:
- Exercise

EMOTIONAL:
- Mindfulness

SPIRITUAL:
- Meditate

WORK:
- Plan my day

FINANCE:
- Track exps

SOCIAL:
- Connect

DATE: **MOOD:** ★ ★ ★ ★ ★

WHAT'S ON MY MIND RIGHT NOW?

GRATITUDE LOG:

MAIN GOALS:

MY AFFIRMATION OF THE DAY...

HAPPINESS CHECKLIST

PHYSICAL:
- Exercise

EMOTIONAL:
- Mindfulness

SPIRITUAL:
- Meditate

WORK:
- Plan my day

FINANCE:
- Track exps

SOCIAL:
- Connect

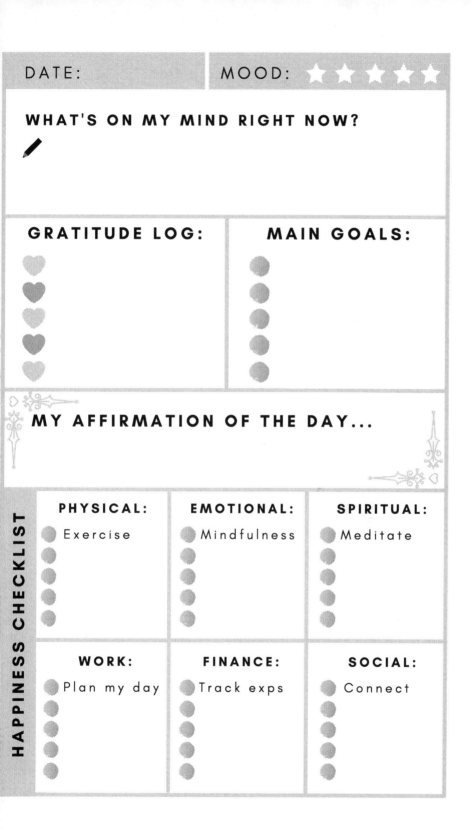

DATE:

MOOD: ⭐ ⭐ ⭐ ⭐ ⭐

WHAT'S ON MY MIND RIGHT NOW?

GRATITUDE LOG:

MAIN GOALS:

MY AFFIRMATION OF THE DAY...

HAPPINESS CHECKLIST

PHYSICAL:
- Exercise
-
-
-
-

EMOTIONAL:
- Mindfulness
-
-
-
-

SPIRITUAL:
- Meditate
-
-
-
-

WORK:
- Plan my day
-
-
-
-

FINANCE:
- Track exps
-
-
-
-

SOCIAL:
- Connect
-
-
-
-

DATE:

MOOD: ★ ★ ★ ★ ★

WHAT'S ON MY MIND RIGHT NOW?

GRATITUDE LOG:

MAIN GOALS:

MY AFFIRMATION OF THE DAY...

HAPPINESS CHECKLIST

PHYSICAL:
- Exercise
-
-
-
-

EMOTIONAL:
- Mindfulness
-
-
-
-

SPIRITUAL:
- Meditate
-
-
-
-

WORK:
- Plan my day
-
-
-
-

FINANCE:
- Track exps
-
-
-
-

SOCIAL:
- Connect
-
-
-
-

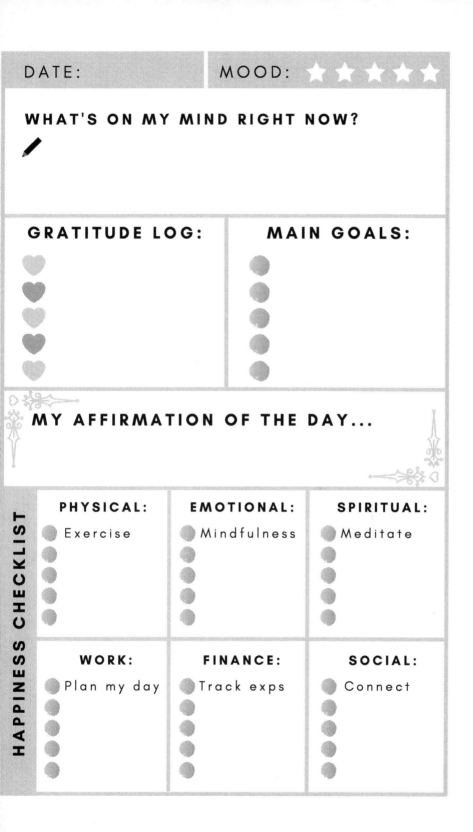

DATE:

MOOD: ★ ★ ★ ★ ★

WHAT'S ON MY MIND RIGHT NOW?

GRATITUDE LOG:

MAIN GOALS:

MY AFFIRMATION OF THE DAY...

HAPPINESS CHECKLIST

PHYSICAL:
- Exercise
-
-
-
-

EMOTIONAL:
- Mindfulness
-
-
-
-

SPIRITUAL:
- Meditate
-
-
-
-

WORK:
- Plan my day
-
-
-
-

FINANCE:
- Track exps
-
-
-
-

SOCIAL:
- Connect
-
-
-
-

DATE: **MOOD:** ★ ★ ★ ★ ★

WHAT'S ON MY MIND RIGHT NOW?

GRATITUDE LOG:

MAIN GOALS:

MY AFFIRMATION OF THE DAY...

HAPPINESS CHECKLIST

PHYSICAL:
- Exercise

EMOTIONAL:
- Mindfulness

SPIRITUAL:
- Meditate

WORK:
- Plan my day

FINANCE:
- Track exps

SOCIAL:
- Connect

DATE: **MOOD:** ⭐ ⭐ ⭐ ⭐ ⭐

WHAT'S ON MY MIND RIGHT NOW?

GRATITUDE LOG:

MAIN GOALS:

MY AFFIRMATION OF THE DAY...

HAPPINESS CHECKLIST

PHYSICAL:
- Exercise
-
-
-
-

EMOTIONAL:
- Mindfulness
-
-
-
-

SPIRITUAL:
- Meditate
-
-
-
-

WORK:
- Plan my day
-
-
-
-

FINANCE:
- Track exps
-
-
-
-

SOCIAL:
- Connect
-
-
-
-

DATE: MOOD: ★ ★ ★ ★ ★

WHAT'S ON MY MIND RIGHT NOW?

GRATITUDE LOG:

MAIN GOALS:

MY AFFIRMATION OF THE DAY...

HAPPINESS CHECKLIST

PHYSICAL:
- Exercise

EMOTIONAL:
- Mindfulness

SPIRITUAL:
- Meditate

WORK:
- Plan my day

FINANCE:
- Track exps

SOCIAL:
- Connect

DATE:

MOOD: ⭐⭐⭐⭐⭐

WHAT'S ON MY MIND RIGHT NOW?

GRATITUDE LOG:

MAIN GOALS:

MY AFFIRMATION OF THE DAY...

HAPPINESS CHECKLIST

PHYSICAL:
- Exercise

EMOTIONAL:
- Mindfulness

SPIRITUAL:
- Meditate

WORK:
- Plan my day

FINANCE:
- Track exps

SOCIAL:
- Connect

WHEEL OF LIFE

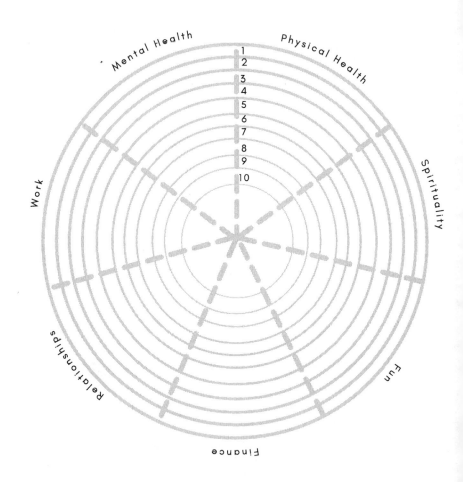

DATE:

Honestly score each of the areas of your life on the wheel based on where you believe you are right now.

Compare the scores of this wheel with your first wheel - how far have you come?

REFLECTIONS

What have I learned so far?

DATE:

REFLECTIONS

What can I do to keep improving my
wheel of life?

DATE:

WELL DONE!

You've finished the 90 day journey of life-improvement, well done!

This is not the end though. If anything, this is just the beginning to a better, happier and more fulfilled life. Even if you put in only a small amount of effort every day over the last 90 days, your life will have improved quite a bit, as your current life score will show. Use this evidence of improvement to celebrate, but also use it to plan your next steps, your ongoing journey of life.

If you want some help with that, consider getting another copy of this workbook, to help guide you for another 90 days. Or better yet, get the 365 day version to keep yourself on track and improving over the course of a year.

Whatever you decide to do, give yourself a pat in the back because you've done well.

All the best with your life, we are rooting for you!

And remember, you've totally got this.

YOU'VE TOTALLY GOT THIS!

Only the
truth of who
you are, if
realized, will
set you free

Eckhart Tolle

Made in the USA
Monee, IL
20 January 2025

10295590R10061